HistoryCaps Presents:

10 Sports Scandals That Rocked the Game

By Frank Foster

BookCaps™ Study Guides

www.bookcaps.com

Table of Contents

About HistoryCaps

HistoryCaps is an imprint of BookCaps™ Study Guides. With each book, a brief period of history is recapped. We publish a wide array of topics (from baseball and music to science and philosophy), so check our growing catalogue regularly (**www.bookcaps.com**) to see our newest books.

Vikings Party Boat Scandal

Spending a wonderful night cruising around on a boat party is a great way for anyone to unwind and enjoy some time on the water with friends. And, just because you are a professional athlete, doesn't mean you can't enjoy those types of luxuries. Just ask some of the players on the Minnesota Vikings in 2005. They were all ready to unwind on the waters and had drawn up a guest list that would ensure a great time was had by all on board. However, minutes into the cruise, it became very clear to the crew that this wasn't a typical cruise or clientele.

The Love Boat

When the crew for the Avanti and Avant Garde, two 64-foot cruising yachts, saw which names were on the guests that would be joining them that night, they were shocked – of the 90 passengers, approximately 30 of them were professional football players for the Minnesota Vikings. It was the middle of the football season for the team, but that week, they didn't have any games so they were ready to take advantage of that free time on their hands. The two yachts were owned and operated by Al and Alma's, a supper club and charter company that frequently hosts cruises on Lake Minnetonka. The company hosts approximately 200 cruises every summer.

On October 6, 2005 during the bye week for the team, dozens of Vikings players and women piled out of their coach limousines and came aboard the two yachts, ready to take part in the annual rookie party. The annual rookie party is a Vikings' tradition. Rookies pay for a night of fun that their older team members delegate. Usually in previous years, the rookie night involves an extravagant dinner and in the more recent years has included a bar or a club. One of the previous rookie nights even involved a stripper in a DJ booth at a local mall after the team ate dinner in a mall restaurant.

The crew was excited and honored to potentially get some time on the boat with some of their favorite players from their very own hometown. Some of the crew was looking forward to the opportunity to even have a chance to take a quick picture with some of the players. However, what they experienced that night was something that they had never expected or even dreamed of.

As the boats left the docks and floated out onto the calm waters of Lake Minnetonka, the wildness that was meant to occur during that night got underway.

It began as a routine cruise for the crewmembers – serving and refilling drinks, serving food and assisting guests whenever it was needed. It was what that crew was hired and paid to do. Many of the crewmembers were young women in their early 20's. However, it was less than a half hour into the ride when they saw the true intentions of their journey that night get underway.

Some of the women that had joined the players on the boat had gone into the bathrooms on the boat and changed their wardrobe into something much less appropriate for a public event. Everything from g-strings to lingerie to nearly nothing at all was not in short supply. It even became clear that some of the women were hired and paid to fly into town to join these players for this event, some of them being strippers.

The women began to grind on the men, removing their clothing, groping on each other and eventually escalating into sex acts being performed out in the open, encouraged and shouted on by onlookers. There was woman on woman action, men on men action and some of the passengers on the cruise even asked members of the crew if they would like to participate in the "fun." Needless to say, it was not quite what the crew had in mind for their evening with a group of professional football players.

The crew was able to identify close to 17 Vikings players that were on the yachts that night; there were four whose names were most associated with the scandal. Mainly, they are some of the most identifiable and well-known players on the team; easy for the crewmembers to remember whom they saw doing what and with whom.

Fred Smoot, corner back, is said to have organized the entire party that night. He allegedly used a purple doubled-headed dildo on two women in front of the other passengers and crewmembers.

Daunte Culpepper, quarterback, received a "lap dance" from an unidentified naked female with inappropriate touching also involved. Moe Williams, running back, is witnessed committing the same acts – lap dance with inappropriate touching.

Bryant McKinnie, offensive tackle, was seen giving oral sex to a woman on top of a bar. He was also seen receiving oral sex while sitting in deck chairs on the boat, along with three other men and three other women.

Not all of the passengers participated in the sex boat activities, but enough information about what went on that night became public knowledge and lead to a police investigation and charges. The captains cut the cruise short and headed back to shore once they had discovered the intent of their journey that night. The passengers filed off the boat leaving behind used condoms, lubricant and sex toys for the crew to clean up. It did not take long for the crew to report what had occurred in front of them.

A Hometown Embarrassment

During the same season that the Love Boat scandal went down, the Vikings were already facing plenty of on and off the field troubles. There was fighting among teammates, embarrassing losses, sexual assault allegations, no hopes at a post-season and even the potential of a new stadium being paid for with the same money used to recruit prospects. Through everything negative that the organization was going through, it was safe to say that the Vikings were spiraling downhill fast. The team was plagued with lack of focus and cohesion on the field, and each and every loss that season made it very clear to the fans and media.

That same year, 2005, Coach Mike Tice was charged for organizing a Super Bowl ticket scalping operation, leading him to be charged with a $100,000 fine. At that time, it was the largest fine handed down to an NFL coach in history. The "Love Boat" scandal most certainly didn't help the team's already hard to win case of positivity in the eye of the public and the media.

Even more embarrassment came when statements from former Vikings players basically said that they were not even being surprised that this type of event occurred. Those former players were more surprised that the event occurred in an extremely public way.

To say that the "Love Boat" scandal was detrimental to the public image and perception of the Vikings is a vast understatement. It didn't matter if a player was on the boat that night or not – the actions of few affected the public image of them all, representing what was supposedly allowed and okay by an organization.

Investigations and Charges

Trials and charges certainly didn't help the reputation crisis that the Minnesota Vikings were facing at that time. The crew of the two yachts that night reported what they had experienced and sparked a criminal investigation into the occurrence. The Hennepin County Sheriff's Office charged the players that were allegedly involved on December 15, a little more than two months after the incident occurred.

The District Court criminal complaints include butt groping, sex toy usage, oral favors, topless lap dances and much more.

Several Vikings players were faced with penalties from the NFL on top of the criminal charges that they were given.

Smoot eventually pled guilty to disorderly conduct and being a public nuisance on a watercraft, being reprimanded with a fine of more than $1,000 and 48 hours of community service. The NFL also levied a hefty fine against Smoot of approximately $82,000. Williams was also fined $300 and 30 hours of community service for indecent conduct, disorderly conduct and lewd or lascivious conduct.

The NFL had no issue levying fines against the Vikings players involved on the Love Boat that night. It is in the contracts with the NFL that players must uphold certain levels of appropriate conduct while they are a player in the league. When they breach those contracts they are faced with game suspensions, fines, community service hours and more, depending on the severity of what they did.

The Vikings found themselves at the butt of every late-night show host's jokes, and to this day face embarrassing questions about that night on the water. Unfortunately for the entire organization and franchise, four players and dozens of others put a nasty black eye on the Vikings organization. Guaranteed, rookie nights from that year forward took a slightly different approach to upholding their team's tradition, one that doesn't end in scandal, investigation, fines and public embarrassment.

2008 Singapore Grand Prix Scandal

At the 2008 Singapore Grand Prix, which is formally known as the Formula 1 SingTel Singapore Grand Prix, the Formula One race seemed to be a typical race day. The 2008 Singapore Grand Prix was the fifteenth race in the Formula One Season and took place at the Marina Bay Street Circuit. For the first time ever, the race was taking place at night. The race was more than 61 laps and was eventually won by Fernando Alonso who was on the Renault team. Nico Rosberg and Lewis Hamilton followed Alonso respectively. However, this race day was far from typical when it came with much scandal.

The Background

It was during the fourteenth lap that Piquet's car crashed, causing major damage during the race. A crash to this nature was almost normal in the high-speed, high-thrill sport. However, this crash was much different than ones that had been seen on the racetrack in the past.

At the time of the crash, Alonso had stopped for both fuel and tires and was off the track. Safety cars were deployed to control the field while the debris that the accident caused was removed from the track. In order for the success of Piquet's planned crash to workout, Alonso was already set with fuel and tires and was able to come out along the front runners of the race following the safety car coming out.

At the end of July, following the Hungarian Grand Prix, Renault fired Piquet. It was prior to that announcement that Piquet Jr. made that his father had warned the FIA that his son wanted to make a statement in regard to the crash that had occurred in Singapore. It was in retaliation for them wanting to tell the truth in which Piquet Jr. and his father believed he had been fired. This brought on many of the reasons that the two let it be known about the conspiracy for the crash from the Singapore Grand Prix.

The entire incident came about when Flavio Briatore and Pat Symonds asked Piquet Jr. to deliberately crash his car in order to help his teammate, Fernando Alonso win the race.

Piquet Jr. said that in the presence of Briatore, Symonds asked him if he would sacrifice his race to benefit Alonso. Piquet Jr. agreed and knew that he needed to crash the car during the 13th or 14th lap of the race and into a wall. Symonds and Briatore went so far so to point out exactly what corner of the track Piquet Jr. should crash into. They knew that there would not be cranes that would help a damaged car easily and swiftly off the track. There were also no side entrances on the track able to easily get a damaged car out of the way. It was the prime location for a crash due to the need for a safety car to be sent onto the track.

Within those conversations of planning out the crash, Piquet Jr. later reported that he felt intense stress and pressure to follow what they were saying because of the threat he felt of not having his contract renewed and being retained on the Renault F1 team for the following year. Piquet Jr. thought that if he followed their instructions, he would have a chance at being retained as a driver in the following year.

With some audio recordings as evidence, along with Alonso being sent to the pit two laps earlier than planned, it seemed that the timing and data proved that the scandal and conspiracy had been set into place as Piquet Jr. reported. The audio that was recorded from radio transmissions from Symonds clearly indicate the instructions given to Alonso to come out to the pit earlier than originally discussed.

Piquet Jr. and his father felt that they were treated extremely poorly by the Renault F1 team when they dared to reveal the scandal and the true meaning behind the crash in Singapore. They knew that there was wrongdoing that damaged the integrity of the sport that they deeply cared about and wanted to do what was necessary to right the wrong. Renault F1 definitely did not want that to happen, and, despite the attacks and threats that they threw at Piquet Jr. and his father, the two still went to the right authorities.

Renault F1 issued a press release prior to court appearances and did all they could to throw Piquet Jr. and his father under the bus. They claimed that Piquet Jr. and his father were lying and that Piquet Jr. actually caused the crash on his own deliberately. They claimed that Piquet Jr. and his father were inventing the lies to blackmail Renault F1 into continuing to let him drive for the team.

The Results

Eventually, the investigation run by the World Motor Sport Council revealed that the allegations that Renault F1 had published in their press release were untrue and unfounded.

The governing body of the FIA asked Renault to answer the charges that the crash that Nelson Piquet Jr. caused was both on purpose, and to assist his teammate Fernando Alonso win the Grand Prix. Renault said that they would not contest the charges. Following the crash and investigation, Renault F1 was given a two-year suspension ban from Formula One due to their involvement in the crash at the Singapore Grand Prix.

The boss of the Renault F1 team, Flavio Briatore, was banned from any FIA-sanctioned races and events for an unlimited period of time. In addition to the ban, any team who was associated with Briatore would not be granted a license by the FIA. Pat Symonds, the former engineering director was also excluded from FIA-sanctioned races and events for five years. Both Briatore and Symonds left the Renault team once the charges were not contested.

Since Piquet was the one who brought the details of the scandal to the proper authorities, he did not face any charges. Alonso, who also went in front of the FIA, was cleared of any possible involvement in race fixing, and was thanked for participating with the authorities.

The World Motor Sport Council found the Renault F1 team guilty of breaking many sporting codes due to their actions. That code included breaches related to the 2008 Singapore Grand Prix to be of unparalleled severity – endangering the lives of many people and compromising the integrity of the sport.

Overall, Renault F1 was extremely cooperative in the entire investigation and took the necessary steps they needed to in order to resolve the failings within their team. Due to that cooperation, the World Motor Sport Council chose to not begin Renault's F1 disqualification until the end of the 2011 season. It was partly due to Renault's internal investigation and their discovery that the only people who were involved in the planned crash were Briatore, Symonds and Piquet Jr. So in the end, although the result was disqualification, they were suspended for two years. This meant that as long as Renault did not mess up again within that time period, they would not face any other problems with the league.

Even with the investigation complete and blame placed, the FIA hearing tried to attribute responsibility to the Singapore scandal even after Briatore and Symonds had gone. However, Renault's own internal investigation was more than enough for the FIA.

Even further, the consequences of the race also had a negative impact on the sales of Renault's cars in the first half of the following year. Within a span of nine months, major car manufacturers, Honda and BMW, pulled out of the F1 race as sponsors.

The Reputation of Renault F1

The planned out crash, the people involved, and the consequences that were felt, were damaging to the reputation of the racing world. As damaging as the scandal was for the racing world, it was just as damaging, if not more, for the Renault F1 team, there was even more damage to the team's reputation. Fans were disgusted at the allegations and revelations behind the crash. There was much nervousness and fear among the Renault F1 team which was understandable considering the allegations and accusations that Piquet Jr. and his father brought to life. No one else on Renault F1 wanted to see themselves go through what Piquet Jr. and his father went through as members of that team, and fear struck strong among them all.

Former three-time world champion Jackie Stewart had plenty to say about the organization and the change that he wanted to see it go through. The quality of leadership and disappointment he felt was made very clear. At the risk of losing commercial sponsors, Renault F1 needed to go through change from the bottom up. The need to redefine their culture, establish responsibility and put quality leadership in place before the organization and reputation of the sport was damaged on a more permanent scale, was more evident than ever during this time period.

Operation Slapshot

In the first ten years of the 21st century, the NHL struggled greatly to get fans to show up to the games. Low attendance, dropping ticket prices and low viewership on television was not a good sign for any professional sports league, but especially not for the NHL, which already struggled to gain acceptance among other popular American sports. In 2004, the league experienced its third lockout between the players and owners that resulted in the first year since 1919 that the Stanley Cup had not been awarded. To say that the public perception and interest was lost on a league and sport that will easily not play its scheduled games due to unnecessary conflict, is an understatement. So in 2006, when even more scandal struck the league, it is safe to say that the repercussions were vast and damaging to the image of the NHL.

The Gambling Ring

James J. Harney was an eight-year police veteran as a New Jersey State Trooper and 40 years old when the suspicions arose regarding his involvement in a large gambling ring that involved many professional sporting events and athletes. At the time the allegations and rumors came to surface, it was said that one of his main partners was Rick Tocchet, an NHL legend.

Tocchet's Background

Rick Tocchet was born April 6, 1964 in Ontario, Canada. In the 1983 NHL Entry Draft, he was picked as number 121 overall, going in the 6th round to the Philadelphia Flyers to play right wing. Tocchet's playing style was quite aggressive as a player and he was known as the enforcer - in the 80's he was known as one of Bruise Brothers with fellow Flyer, Dave Brown.

Tocchet was a member of the Philadelphia Flyers until 1991-1992 when he joined the Pittsburgh Penguins. During his time with the Flyers, he played in the Stanley Cup Finals in 1987. Once he joined the Penguins in 1992, Tocchet joined the team in dominating the playoffs, and was finally able to take a sip from his first Stanley Cup.

Throughout the rest of his time in the NHL as a player, Tocchet spent several years with the Los Angeles Kings, the Boston Bruins, the Washington Capitals and the Phoenix Coyotes until he joined the Philadelphia Flyers to play with them again. Tocchet retired as a player in 2002 as a Philadelphia Flyer, the very same way that he began his career.

Tocchet did have a successful career as a player despite being a member of several different teams for brief amounts of time. In 1,144 NHL games, Tocchet totaled 440 goals and 512 assists. He also totaled 2,972 penalty minutes. Tocchet was picked and received the opportunity to play in four NHL All-Star Games in 1989, 1990, 1991 and 1993.

Once his time was up as a player and Tocchet retired, he went on to try his coaching skills as an assistant coach for the Colorado Avalanche from 2002-2004. Then, in the 2005-2006 season, Tocchet was an assistant coach for the Phoenix Coyotes. From that season, Tocchet became an assistant coach for the Tampa Bay Lightning in 2008-2009. During the 2008-2009 season, Tocchet was a mid-season replacement and was named head coach for the Lightning. He was also the head coach the following season. Tocchet met Harney in a south Philadelphia sports bar in the 1990s and began the ring in 2001.

Another key player in the ring and the investigation, and a lot of the reason that this story had so much publicity was Wayne Gretzky. Granted, it was not Gretzky's actions that were the reason his name was popping up in the media in association with the scandal. Gretzky's wife, actress Janet Jones, was accused on being involved in the gambling ring as well. Tocchet was accused of placing bets for Jones.

The other main person involved in the gambling ring was James Ulmer. Ulmer was said to be the "sitter" who would get the wages to Harney. He was not a professional athlete or law enforcement officer, so there was not much public focus on his portion of the gambling ring.

The Investigation

Everyone is innocent until proven guilty in the United States of America, and as guilty as the public felt Tocchet and the other players in the ring were, the investigation was going to truly reveal what was going on.

It took an extremely long time for the New Jersey State Police to investigate the nationwide sports gambling ring because of the complexity of the case and those who were involved. It is during that investigation that the term, Operation Slap Shot, was born. Part of the naming was due to the need for some of the investigation to be done undercover to truly figure out who the key players were.

During Operation Slap Shot, it was found that more than 1,000 wagers exceeding nearly $1.7 million total were processed in a 40-day period. All of the bets and wagers were put on professional and college sports, specifically football and basketball. From the Super Bowl to college bowl games, the ring had money exchanged and wagered.

Since Tocchet was a hockey coach and a member of Wayne Gretzky's staff for the Phoenix Coyotes, there was a lot of suspicion around whether or not there was any betting on hockey. The suspicion also came around from if it was NHL players who were making those bets. In the investigation, they were also checking for any illegalities committed by the bettors in regard to who they were and what they were betting on.

New Jersey State Police Superintendent, Col. Rick Fuentes, did state that none of the bets made by NHL players were bet on hockey. However, it was confirmed that approximately 12 people who either associated with an NHL club or were actually a part of an NHL club, took part in the nationwide gambling ring. This included a team owner, member of a coaching staff and Tocchet himself. Those who participated in the gambling ring were located all around the country and Canada. The ring was fairly evident in south New Jersey and Philadelphia area.

Once the allegations were brought to light, Tocchet was on leave from his coaching responsibilities. Harney, a trooper for eight years, was also put on suspension from his responsibilities. Two state troopers were also suspended without pay for knowing that the ring existed yet failing to report it to the proper authorities. Ulmer was said to have been the sitter in the entire operation.

The investigation resulted in charges ultimately being brought against Harney, Tocchet and Ulmer.

The Charges

For his large role in the gambling ring, Officer Harney was charged with second-degree conspiracy, second-degree official misconduct and third-degree of promoting gambling. James Ulmer was charged with promoting gambling, money laundering and conspiracy.

Harney faced seven years in prison, and eventually pleaded guilty after testifying against Tocchet and Ulmer. He forfeited more than $700,000 in property, cash, watches and plasma televisions. Since he was a part of the police force as a trooper and had clearly broken the law, he was on unpaid suspension from his $74,500 job following his arrest that February. Harney eventually resigned from the force, completely embarrassed. His original sentence was held at 25 years, and, had they gone to trial, most likely would've held.

He penned a letter with his most sincere apologies and his confession of a lapse of judgment which was posted on his lawyer's website. Harney also stated in the letter that he apologized for the humiliation and disgrace that he brought to the Division of State Police.

Tocchet was the most high-profile suspect in the entire operation and investigation – an NHL player who was accused of betting on his own sport, team and players. While the other two ring leaders were charged and pleaded guilty, Tocchet wasn't indicted by a grand jury. Nearly a year had passed since the charges and accusations were brought to light and Tocchet still hadn't been charged, causing legal experts to suggest that there simply wasn't enough evidence, a problem with the evidence or the case was too complex.

Gretzky and his wife threatened the State of New Jersey with a $50 million defamation suit because the allegations against her were found false. In the state of New Jersey, it was not illegal to bet through a bookie, so even if some of the allegations were true, there wouldn't be any legal ramifications. It is not even illegal to place a bet. However, it was proven that Gretzky knew about the gambling ring through secretly recorded phone conversations through law enforcement forces.

The entire Operation Slapshot put a major black eye on the face of not only the NHL, but also the New Jersey State Police Department and all of their operations. From the accusations to the investigation to the charges, it was made clear that this kind of behavior wasn't going to be tolerated at all by anyone, anywhere – whether they were an athlete or law enforcement officer.

Bundesliga Scandal

Soccer is undoubtedly one of the most popular sports on the earth. From the spectators to the players who dedicate their lives - each country sings praise and love at all levels of the sport. No matter what you call the sport, soccer or futbol, there is immense respect for the game and for those who play, ensuring the strong importance that rules must be followed. In 2005, the German Football Association (DFB) and the Bundesliga, were at the center of the soccer world under immense scrutiny and embarrassment. It was the allegations that members of the association were betting on and fixing matches that led to the association's and league's second scandal in 50 years.

The First Time Around

When scandal about cheating and betting on game outcomes came to light in 2005, it certainly wasn't the first time that a scandal had come to light within this league. Bundesliga history has another very dark chapter in its past with the discovery of a very large scale match fixing scheme in the 1970's.

In the 1970's, a very complex match fixing scheme was completely revealed when Offenbach's President Horst-Gregorio Canellas hit play on an audio tape following the end of the 1970-71 season during a party with his team. The audiotape revealed recordings of the very conversations that held the fate of the soccer games, fates that were decided before a second of play was even played, before a single ball was kicked. Canellas had had a conversation with a defender who played for Berlin, and in that conversation, it was revealed that they were paid to lose in a very surprising loss against Bielefeld. It was because of that loss, that Offenbach had been relegated and no longer had a spot in the Bundesliga. Berlin had gone with the outcome of the highest bidder, Bielefeld where each player was offered 15,000 German marks or $9,000 for the loss from Bielefeld.

Also in attendance at Canellas' party were league officials and journalists who helped to both investigate the incident and spread the news that cheating and conspiracy had indeed taken place during controversial matches. Two Berlin players, Bernd Patzke and Tasso Wild, were found to have been contributing factors to the loss against Bielefeld, and that the fixed match came down to a team vote in the locker room prior to the game starting.

It was also revealed that the game between Bielefeld and Berlin was not the only game that had been fixed that season. Bielefeld offered many teams incentive to lose matches and provide an outcome that was ideal for either their team or their wallets. The league had a salary cap of 1,200 marks a month, which made it very appeasing for the players to entertain the thought of getting some extra cash on the side just for throwing a match or two.

Overall, about 60 players, coaches and managers were involved in some aspect of fixing matches in Bundesliga club games. Bielefeld and Offenbach lost their licenses in the Bundesliga. More importantly, the league lost fans. Shocked and horrified at the dishonesty of their teams, many German soccer fans turned their back on the sport. Stadiums were difficult to fill and the teams rarely saw support. It was not until the Germans won the World Cup in 1974 in Germany that fans began to give the sport another chance. Many anti-corruption and ethical standards were included in league rules to prevent anything like this from happening again. That was until 2005.

Second Time Around

In 2005, corruption and dishonesty in the league all began again with the accusations surrounding referee Robert Hoyzer. Hoyzer was 25 years old at the time and had been a referee since 2001. Growing up, his father was also a referee. Hoyzer worked his way up through the Bundesliga but was never able to make it to the 1st Bundesliga.

One match was in the center of all of the scandal. Following the defeat of second division Hamburg SV, 4-2 by regional side SC Paderborn, Hoyzer was under suspicion for fixing the match. One of the matches Hoyzer is suspected of betting on was a German cup tie between Hamburg and Paderborn. Paderborn was lower-ranked than Hamburg, making the loss slightly suspicious. During the game, Hoyzer sent off a Hamburg player, striker Émile Mpenza, and gave Paderborn two penalties.

Following those allegations, several referees were pulled from their matches because they were suspected to have been involved. Those referees included Juergen Jansen, Felix Zwayer and Dominik Marks. Jansen was one of the biggest surprises because he is commonly assigned the matches in the Bundesliga's top division. Zwayer and Marks ended up being under investigation for fixing ten matches.

As it was suspected that he was involved in fixing matches and following much scrutiny, Hoyzer finally publically admitted that all of the speculation was indeed true, that he had participated in fixing matches within the Bundesliga. In his full-blown cooperation with the investigators, Hoyzer admitted everything he knew regarding the match fixing. This included other games, players and coaches in which Hoyzer ended up revealing to the state prosecutors.

Hoyzer Wasn't Alone

With admitting his guilt and throughout all of the findings and speculation, it became more and more clear that Hoyzer was definitely not acting alone in fixing matches. Following the admission of his own guilt, Hoyzer told the prosecutors the other people who had played a role in fixing Bundesliga matches.

Simply by beginning with Hoyzer, the accusations and allegations spread to a total of 25 people who were suspected of manipulating 10 soccer matches. There were 14 players who were among the 25 people suspected of playing roles in fixing matches.

Following his arrest, Hoyzer was generous with giving information to the proper authorities about specifically who else they should be interested in getting information from – leading to the arrest of Dominik Marks. Even more so after Hoyzer was giving out information, it became clear that the match fixing could've possibly gone all the way up to the UEFA headquarters, with cheating and gambling occurring during instances such as the UEFA Champions League and the UEFA Cup.

The Findings

Once Hoyzer admitted to fixing matches, the investigation was extremely thorough in discovering exactly which matches were affected. Overall, Hoyzer was involved in fixing seven cup and lower league matches. Not only did the investigation find that there was fixing within the Bundesliga, but also in other clubs. Lower division clubs involved with fixing matches included Dresden and Chemnitz, both clubs that had been mentioned in match fixing with referee Jurgen Jansen.

Included in the Bundesliga side of the scandal was Hertha Berlin. Three of Hertha Berlin's players Alexander Madlung, Nando Rafael and Josip Simunic, were all found to be connected with the second round match between Hertha and Eintracht Braunschweig. Braunschweig won the second round match 3-2 over Hertha when Braunschweig's own defender scored on their own goal to ensure Hertha's defeat.

Also found in the investigation was that the captain from Paderborn, Thijs Waterink, received 10,000 euros as an incentive to defeat Hamburg in the match for the cup tie, coming from an anonymous backer. With Hoyzer's assistance, Paderborn did win and the unrecorded bonuses were split among the victorious Paderbon teammates.

Hoyzer's lawyer raised some criticism in the way the investigation was handled along with the consequences for Hoyzer, saying that Hoyzer was forced into signing a resignation letter from refereeing and the game. Overall, the results of Hoyzer's actions resulted in him being jailed for more than two years, a major relief from the original criminal sentence of ten years. Dominik Marks was convicted for his role in the scheme and jailed for a year and a half.

Because of the actions of Hoyzer and all involved, the DFB adopted new policies and procedures to prevent any additional instances such as this from occurring again. Initially for the 2005 – 2006 season, all betting on football matches was banned for anyone associated with the sport. The ban included players, coaches, referees and officials. The DFB also changed their notification process for referees, making it four days prior to a game instead of too far in advance.

Beyond all of the rumors at the beginning of the investigation, one thing was for sure: there is indeed corruption in one of the world's most beloved sports. Knowing when that corruption is evident takes someone brave enough to unearth the truth, and those who are guilty admitting their wrongdoing. Throughout all that was uncovered, it became even clearer that that corruption went much higher up than anyone cared to admit, or wanted to hear and believe.

Hoyzer sat in jail, attempting to change the sentence that he had been dealt for his actions but ultimately paid the price for cheating. The sport of soccer, and specifically the Bundesliga, certainly had a lot of damage control to do and image repair to focus on in the years following yet another cheating scandal.

Black Sox Scandal

The World Series. One of the most coveted championships in all of sports. Teams represent two nationwide leagues, the American and National, and throughout the entire baseball season, work to have the opportunity to play for it all. Players represent their city, teammates, coaches, family and even more so, themselves.

To reach the top of your sport is a prestigious honor. After years and years of practice and preparation, countless sacrifices and setbacks, reaching the top is an opportunity that should never be taken lightly.

However, in 1919, a major controversy tainted the tradition of this sport and changed the game forever.

The Set-up

The record reflects that the Cincinnati Reds were crowned World Series champions, winning the eighth game against the Chicago White Sox. Regardless of how many games it took, that is exactly what the record was going to reflect, the Reds being crowned World Champions, before the first pitch was even thrown out in Game 1.

The conspiracy to rig the World Series was developed among eight members of the Chicago White Sox after well-known gamblers and bookies approached them. The gamblers and bookies approached some of those players individually while others were approached by their own teammates. Some of the White Sox players happened to catch wind by eavesdropping on conversations about the fix among those who were already involved. It was going to take a true group effort to throw an entire World Series and the people placing the bets wanted to ensure their money would not go to waste.

Back in that time, it was common for the players to bet on games, and the fans were just as much a part of the game as the players were, investing their hard earned cash with the hope that it would pay off big when the odds went in their favor. During that time, baseball owners were extremely tight with their money and sometimes so much so that players struggled with their income and living expenses. It was hard for some players to turn away from a chance at nearly $20,000 to fix the outcome of a game when the players were making so little - the gamblers knew their struggle and thrived on it.

The entire season, the starting lineup of the White Sox was promising: people knew that that team had the potential to go the distance and win the entire World Series. It was going to be easy money. It was such easy money, that the bets on the White Sox to win it all were rolling in. The experienced gamblers, the ones who knew how to make things go their way, saw that opportunity and knew what they had to do. Convince the Sox to throw it, and they would come out on top bigger than they ever had before.

Of course, the gamblers weren't the only ones who would benefit from fixing the World Series. The players involved were promised roughly $100,000 total among them for throwing the Series.

The Key Players

Before the game started, there were bets being made on the outcome of the game - just like they have always done with any sporting event.

Sport was a well-known bookmaker and gambler, a name that is one of the biggest associated with the scandal. He summoned first baseman Chuck Gandil prior to the World Series about how games should play out, confident that they could fix the series the way they wanted. Gandil, one of the biggest names associated with the fix, was a professional baseball player and member of the Chicago White Sox. He began playing professionally in 1908, and was later known as one of the best first basemen in the league. He was sold to the White Sox in 1917 for $3,500.

Gandil and his co-conspirator, Eddie Cicotte, told Sullivan they would think it over. Six other players also became involved in the plan to fix the outcome of the World Series. Pitcher Claude Williams, outfielders Joe Jackson and Happy Felsch, shortstop Swede Risberg, reserve Fred McMullin, and third baseman Buck Weaver.

Charles Comiskey, the owner of the White Sox, was not very popular among the players. He had a reputation in the league for underpaying his players compared to the rest of the teams in the league at that time, easily fueling the players' desire to make a little bit of extra cash.

How it Went Down

In a best of nine series, there was a lot of different ways for the White Sox to throw the game. Game 1 of the series was at Redland Field, home of the Cincinnati Reds. Gandil had told Sullivan that he wanted to be paid up front, something that Sullivan couldn't deliver but one that Arnold Rothstein could. Before the start of the first game, Cicotte found $10,000 under his pillow – a clear sign that the fix was on from a financial standpoint, and that it was up to the players to hold up their end.

During the first game of the series, a pitch from Cicotte hit the first batter on the Reds – signaling that the fix was on.

By throwing the first game, 9-1, the players on the White Sox were supposed to earn $10,000. No money came. The same thing was supposed to happen when the White Sox threw the second game. When the White Sox lost the second game, 4-2, the players were given only $10,000 of the $40,000 that they were owed.

The players were fed up and betrayed since they had not yet received the money that they were owed. Deciding to do the right thing after all, the eight players decided to play the next game to the best of their ability. The White Sox won the third game of the series 3-0, leaving Sullivan extremely unhappy. Since the White Sox won, Sullivan finally came up with the $20,000 that was owed to the players before Game 4 with more money coming if they continued with the fix that they had agreed upon.

Gandil took that $20,000 and split it up between Risberg, Felsch, Williams and Jackson, leaving out McMullin and Weaver. The rest of the $20,000 of the original $40,000 that is owed to the players was given to them when they lost game 4 and then game 5. That same $20,000 never came so again, the White Sox gave their all and won game 6, 5-4 and game 7, 4-1.

Going into Game 8, it was a tied series. Lefty Williams was the starting pitcher and the game was downhill from the start – the Reds scored four runs in the first inning alone. The Cincinnati Reds won the 1919 World Series in game 8, 10-5 over the Chicago White Sox. The fix had been made. Dollars had been dispersed and it was time to move onto the next prize.

All the Controversy

About a year after the World Series, the conspiracy between the Sox and gamblers to fix the outcome of the game became public knowledge. The eight members involved in the conspiracy became known as the Black Sox. Once the controversy broke, it was unclear who was involved, when they were involved and more. The multiple sides to the story, especially with eight members of the team being involved, makes it hard to determine the entire truth. When the conspirators were on trial, Cicotte and Jackson admitted their part in the conspiracy; Gandil, however, didn't admit anything.

The questionable trial resulted in acquittals for all accused of being involved. Although the court wasn't able to levy down the proper punishments, the eight players involved in the fix were not out of the woods. Commissioner Kenesaw Mountain Landis gave them all lifetime suspensions.

Some of the biggest controversy and disappointment among the fans came from the involvement of Joe Jackson. One of the American Leagues best players at the time, Jackson consistently denied his involvement in fixing the game. Although he was banned from the game because of the perception that he was involved, Jackson always points to the records and statistics from that Series – proving that he really did give his all and that his stats were comparable with the rest of his performance all season.

Even more controversy and questions arose over the involvement of Comiskey. He claims that he had no knowledge of the fix while the gamblers and players claim that he in fact was aware of the plan.

The Black Sox

They weren't the Chicago White Sox that the Windy City had loved; this team was a dark cloud hanging over the loved traditions of a great sport. Forever tainting that World Series with a black cloud of distrust, the nicknamed Chicago Black Sox handed the Cincinnati Reds a World Championship for a price of $100,000. The lies, the truths, conspiracies and dollars exchanged among the crooked and the players altered professional baseball in that time period forever. To this day, it is still a controversy with more questions left unanswered than answered – a controversy that helped shape the culture of America's beloved pastime.

Baylor University Basketball Scandal

Crisis and controversy go very much hand in hand when they strike. A crisis can cause a controversy, and controversies can very much cause a crisis. Baylor University's men's basketball team saw the truth of that impact that crisis and controversy can have on more than just a basketball season. This was about more than who is going to be the starting line up or who was the new team leader in scoring – this came down to murder, lies, cheating, drugs, secret tapes and a full-blown cover up. The scars that came down on the men's program at Baylor University in 2003 will forever be engrained in college basketball.

The Murder

Patrick Dennehy was missing for six weeks before his body was found. A McLennan County deputy discovered Dennehy's body a few miles southeast of Baylor's campus, barely recognizable by those who saw him last. A tragic ending to a life taken way too soon.

Dennehy was born in Santa Clara, California and he came to play for Baylor's men's basketball team after transferring from University of New Mexico. Due to NCAA rules, Dennehy had to be redshirted in the 2002-2003 season and could not play right away. Dennehy became eligible to play for the 2003-2004 season. His future as a college basketball player was bright, a very promising member of Baylor's team with a potential shot at a professional career.

Carlton Dotson was also a transfer student and came to Baylor during the summer of 2002. Dotson and Dennehy were fairly close friends. They had bonded over their love for music and the sport of basketball, and had even lived together as roommates. The two had also bonded over their love of shooting pistols and practiced frequently together at a range north of their campus. After the two didn't show up to a party that they were supposed to attend, and Dennehy's parents had not heard from him for several days, suspicions and concerns began to arise.

On June 19, an official missing person's report was filed for Dennehy after he had not been heard from for several days. On July 25, nearly six weeks after Dennehy had gone missing, his body was found.

The autopsy revealed that Dennehy had been shot twice, above his right ear and behind his head, clearly revoking the possibility that Dotson shot Dennehy out of self-defense, something that the defense had tried to prove. Dotson had fled to Maryland to try and out run his crimes, seeking refuge from family and tossing the murder weapon out along the way there.

After initially denying his guilt of murdering Dennehy, on June 8, Dotson pleaded guilty to killing Dennehy just five days before the trial was supposed to start. After a fairly brief trial, Dotson was sentenced to 35 years in prison for the murder of his former Baylor teammate. Much of the disturbing part of the case was Dotson's insistence that there were voices in his head and that he suffered from paranoia that people were trying to kill him. He also believed that he was Jesus, the Son of God.

Dotson was sent to a state mental hospital and at one point, found incompetent to stand trial. He was prescribed anti-psychotic medication following the recommendations of a hospital psychologist, but Dotson's attorneys did not pursue the insanity defense.

It was after the death of Dennehy that allegations of NCAA violations began to surface about the Baylor program. Cheating, lying, financial dishonesty and more turned from whispers into shouts and the NCAA had no choice but to investigate.

A Failed Cover-up & Extreme Controversy

Despite head coach Dave Bliss' extreme insistence, Baylor University's men's basketball program was far from clean. The corruption and cheating that occurred in the program were by far some of the worst that had been seen in a college program in years. But for Baylor University, this was a road that they had traveled on before; the men's basketball scandal was the second basketball scandal at the university in the past ten years, and the third total athletic scandal. In 2000, the men's tennis program was penalized for improper financial aid and extra benefits being given.

The lack of a clean program at Baylor is evident on all levels, especially from a history standpoint, but if you asked its coach, he had been running clean programs for more than 30 years.

It took a matter of weeks for an internal investigation at Baylor to find that Coach Bliss had been directly involved in paying for both Dennehy and another player's tuition and other expenses, up to a total of almost $40,000. During the NCAA investigation, Bliss admitted to those illegal payments to the two players, but only after he had attempted to cover-up the real truth – the truth that clearly displayed his illegal involvement. He also solicited nearly $87,000 from Baylor boosters improperly per NCAA standards.

Once it was discovered that Dennehy had been killed, Bliss went around to the assistant coaches and players to have them feed the story to anyone who asked that Dennehy had received extra cash because he was dealing drugs. To thwart Bliss' plan in its tracks, assistant coach Abar Rouse recorded what Bliss was saying to the players and other coaches. Bliss was making the players and coaches practice what they were going to say when approached about the situation, coaching them through the answers that he thought would be best at saving a program he loved, with no concern for moral obligations.

Rouse was extremely uncomfortable with what Bliss was asking him to do and turned over the recordings he had taken to the local media, leading to multiple publications and stories, along with plenty of local media coverage. Bliss resigned as coach of Baylor's men's basketball team on August 8.

Not only was the program plagued with illegal financing, but the NCAA investigation also found that failed drug tests by the players were not properly reported as required.

Bliss was a desperate coach – he couldn't let the corruption in his program destroy his reputation, and he felt that it was his reputation of running clean programs that would save him in the end. He was greatly mistaken. Bliss' attempt at a cover-up at the expense of a man, his own player, who was killed, is one that destroyed every second of positive reputation he had built up during his thirty-year career. Maybe if he had been truthful from the start, the outcome of the scandal may have been different, but that is one that Bliss can debate in his mind every single day from now on.

The NCAA

The NCAA, the governing body of college athletics that puts the best interests of the student-athlete at the heart of their mission, was swift to levy down punishments at Baylor once they investigated the program. The investigation was sparked by the murder of Dennehy, and much more was unearthed in their findings. Harsh penalties were handed down to Baylor as a result of the NCAA's investigation. In the summer of 2005, two years after the death of Dennehy, Baylor was facing the death penalty – a fair price for a repeat offender.

Baylor was allowed to choose which of two upcoming seasons they would not play the regularly scheduled non-conference games, which is typically 15 total games per season. Baylor was still eligible for in-conference play and the post season. The NCAA put the program on probation for five years, from 2005-2010.

Due to further infractions and cover-ups that the NCAA found, Baylor's levied some self-imposed penalties. Baylor put itself on three years of probation, reduced scholarships and minimized the contact that was allowed between coaches and recruits. All players were additionally offered a release from their scholarships, allowing them the opportunity to transfer as necessary without having to sit out the usually required season. Ultimately, the school banned itself from postseason play in the 2003-2004 season.

The NCAA, feeling that Baylor's own sanctions were fair, did not end up giving the program the death penalty, although, the NCAA did extend Baylor's reductions and recruiting visits between coaches and players were extended by a year.

Three of Baylor's star players left that season for other schools: Lawrence Roberts to Mississippi State, John Lucas III to Oklahoma State, and Kenny Taylor to Texas. The program was crippled that season, and for good reason.

Moving Forward

What occurred at Baylor University in the men's basketball program set a precedent for college athletics. A scandal with continuous twists and turns clearly showed how corrupted a program can be. In the 2006-2007 season, Baylor gained back their scholarships and was eligible for all of their games throughout the season. Although the program continued to move on and the players did as well, it is hard to forget how detrimental the corruption in an athletics program can be on an entire school.

Baylor University as a whole had to pick itself back up, define who they were and move on from the terrible scandal and tragedy that occurred at their school.

2000 Paralympic Games

Founded in 1989, the Paralympics have created an amazing opportunity for athletes with impairment to compete at the sports that they love from beginner to elite levels. The vision of the Paralympics is to enable by creating conditions for athlete empowerment, primarily focus on Paralympic athletes from initiation to elite level, achieve sporting excellence and to inspire and excite by touching the heart of all people for a more equitable society. The stories and performance of the athletes who compete inspire our societies on a local and national level with the goal of contributing to a more equal society filled with respect and equal opportunity for all. In 2000, that wonderful, honest mission and vision faced a huge cheating scandal.

2000 Summer Games

The 2000 Summer Paralympic Games were held in Sydney, Australia. There were 3,881 female and male Paralympic athletes who represented a total of 122 countries in the world. During the games, a record total of 1.2 million tickets were sold for people to watch the athletes compete. More than 2,300 media representatives were present and the games could be broadcasted online, which allowed viewers in more than 103 countries to watch the games from afar, no matter where they were in the world. The website had more than 300 million hits throughout all of the competition at the games that year.

On October 18, 2000, the Olympic Games got underway and the athletes competed in a total of 18 sports. This was the first year that the Paralympic Games had wheelchair rugby as one of their sports. The USA won against Australia in the gold medal final, 32-21. In the spirit of the Paralympics, celebrating the amazing success of the athletes who compete, several athletes gave outstanding personal performances.

These Olympic Games were also the first year for the women's power lifting event. Jianxin Bian of China and Fatma Omar of Egypt won the first two gold medals in this sport. British wheelchair athlete Tanni Grey-Thompson won four gold medals in the 100m, 200m, 400m, and 800m races, respectively.

Jason Wening was born with deformities in his legs for no apparent medical reason. At the age of 3, Wening had double below the knee amputations on his legs. Throughout his childhood, he had a supportive family who strived to make his life as normal as possible. He grew up in an environment that consistently showed him the respect and equality that every human deserves, no matter how different they may be.

It was while his father was stationed in the military in Heidelberg, Germany that Wening's passion for swimming really developed and his career took off. Swimming frequently was especially helpful as a part of Wening's therapeutic recovery, due to a surgical operation that was needed to correct a deformity in his left hip.

It was because of his passion for swimming that Wening truly developed his academic passions and field of study as well. Wening attended and graduated from the University of Michigan, earning his Ph.D. by studying the biomechanics of the human shoulder. This area of academia was an area that he developed interest in because of his swimming career. He wanted to really get an understanding of the way shoulders worked and how the joints operated during a physical activity, which could carry over into swimming.

Studying hard was not the only thing that Wening filled his time with while he was in school. He trained six days a week, swimming approximately 11,000 meters a day and worked out on dry land to prepare for the Paralympics in Sydney to defend his previous records.

Wening's hard work paid off, and that year at the 2000 Sydney Summer Paralympic Games, he won his third consecutive gold medal in the 400m Freestyle, breaking his own world record – a record he set and has continue to beat since 1991.

These are just a few of the amazing stories that are seen from the athletes who compete in the Paralympics. What they overcome to do what they love to do is an inspiration to all.

To even dream that anyone would damage that genuine spirit that brings equality to us all, is a difficult thing to do but that year, Spain's men's basketball team broke those odds.

Cheating Spain

The Spanish men's basketball team dominated their competition. It was fairly easy for them to get to the gold medal match, taking on the men's team from Russia. Throughout the tournament, the Spanish team had zero losses. They won the semi-finals against Poland 97-67 and went on to beat Russia in the finals, 87-63. Gold medals hung proudly around the necks of the athletes, and the sponsorship dollars were rolling in strong.

That was of course until their entire scheme was exposed.

It was, thanks to the exposé published by Spanish undercover journalist Carlos Ribagorda, that the dishonesty of the Spanish men's basketball team was even discovered. Ribagorda had been covering the team and investigating two years prior to the 2000 Summer Paralympic Games in Sydney. Ribagorda attended sporadic training sessions to get an inside look at the training that occurred for the Paralympic atheletes.

To determine eligibility to play in the intellectually disabled category at the Paralympics, the only test that Ribagorda was required to take was to do six press-ups and then have his blood pressure taken. Of the 12 athletes on the Spanish men's basketball team, only two of them actually had intellectual disabilities. Also thanks to his insider perspective, Ribagroda reported 15 of the 200 total athletes on the Spanish Paralympic team did not have intellectual disabilities as required by the IPC. The Spanish men's basketball team was stripped of their gold medals.

Prior to the cheating being exposed, Spain had finished third overall in the medal count at the Sydney 2000 Games. They fell behind Australia and Britain with a total of 107 medals, with 38 of them being gold. The athletes for the men's basketball team, along with a few other sports, were chosen by the Spanish Federation for Mentally Handicapped Sports so that they could easily win more medals and gain more sponsorship.

The Spanish team not only fooled and failed the country that they were chosen to represent, but they also unfairly competed against athletes who were actually intellectually disabled.

The Backlash

Two months after it came to light what the Spanish had done in the 2000 Sydney Paralympic Games, the International Paralympic Committee (IPC) ended up banning athletes with intellectual disabilities, realizing that a new system needed to be put in place to eliminate the possibility of unfair competition.

Investigations, resignations and more all took place after the cheating was exposed. A total of 18 people, including players on the Spanish men's basketball team and managers of the Spanish Federation for Mentally Handicapped Sports (FEDDI) were charged for their part in the cheating scandal at the games. The court in Madrid ended up dropping the charges.

The architect of the entire scandal, Fernando Martin Vicente, was fined by a Spanish court for a total of approximately $7,766 for his part in the cheating scandal. Fernando Martin Vicente, who was the head of the FEDDI, was also ordered to return $204,728 that he had helped distribute to the players that were not actually eligible to receive the government funding that they had previously been given because they were not disabled athletes. Martin Vicente publicly apologized for his part in the cheating scandal and officially resigned prior to the findings from the investigation being released to the public.

Present State

In 2012, at the London Paralympic Games, some of the previously removed intellectually disabled events were restored, but not all of them. Adding these events back in opened up the possibility for those athletes with an intellectual disability, who had been excluded due to the actions of the Spanish men's basketball team, to finally have a chance to compete again. Some intellectually disabled athletes did not feel it was fair to be punished for the crimes of one country, but have the hope that the playing field will be fair from now on, making an example out of Spain.

Additionally, the paranoia that other teams could try to cheat the system once again does exist, but one would hope that there really was a valuable lesson learned, and that an example was made by the dishonesty and cheating that Spanish did in 2000.

There are still plenty of questions that remain among the Paralympics' athletes, media and spectators of the Paralympic Games – is it really fair for intellectually disabled athletes to compete? That is just one of the many questions that the IPC and host countries must weigh as they determine what sports to have available at their games.

The values of the Paralympics include courage, determination, inspiration and equality. It is the hope that every athlete who has the opportunity to represent their country doing the sport that they love, will uphold those values to the best of their ability and at all times.

Tokitsukaze Stable

The invincibility of athletes can sometimes make the public unaware of what is going on behind the scenes. Athletes are strong and they have risen above the rest to prove that they have the right skills to compete at the highest levels of their sport. Throughout the world, different cultures celebrate different sports and the athletes who train hours on hours to compete in them. In Japan, sumo wrestling is highly regarded as one of the greatest. The training and dedication that it takes to become a successful sumo wrestler are parallel to those of other sports. Since 1989, four wrestlers had died from a supposed heart failure of one way or another during their training. In 2007, the world saw once again just how damaging the sport of wrestling in Japan could actually be.

The Devastation

The Tokitsukaze stable is a stable of sumo wrestlers in Japan. Previously known as Futabayama, which is the namesake of the wrestler at the time, the stable of Tokisukaze was named in 1945 when Futabayama retired. Tokisukaze was the name of the wrester and coach who was in charge of the stable.

In Japan, sumo wrestlers all belong to a stable, which is very similar to a gym or dormitory. All sumo wrestlers live and train together and all under the supervision of the stable master. All of the stable masters worked as a group, and therefore, they were collective owners of the Japan Sumo Association. They worked with each other to create the governance and legislation for their league, seeing that rules are followed and altered when situations arise. They received payments from the national association for every wrestler that they had in their stable. It is that financial attachment to the wrestlers that caused the stable wrestlers to put extreme pressure on their students to succeed, their own paychecks depended on it.

Takashi Saito, was a young junior wrestler who was brought in to learn and train with Junichi Yamamoto, who was a stable master. There were many common training practices and grueling schedules that the wrestlers needed to stick to. When they stepped out of line, there were definitely consequences, and many stables had their own unique practices to dealing with necessary punishments. Baseball bats were common in training for sumo wrestlers, but not in the way that Saito had ever imagined. It was following a beating that Saito collapsed and died after a training session at Tokitsukaze stable's lodgings in Inuyama.

The reasoning behind Saito's beating was due to the perception from stable master Yamamoto and some of the other wrestlers that Saito had an unacceptable and vague attitude about his career in sumo wrestling. An attitude such as that was seen as extremely poor and was not only frowned upon by Yamamoto, but also by the other wrestlers that he trained with and throughout the culture of the sport in general.

When Saito collapsed, people were shocked, and as the news spread, many shrugged off the incident. Their lack of concern for the incident was originally due to the death of the young wrestler being reported and ruled the result of a heart failure. That reporting settled the matter for some people and they moved on, but Saito's father knew that there was something more than that causing the death of his son. At first, the police were reluctant to do a thorough investigation into the cause of Saito's death despite the numerous bruises, cuts and burns that were evident on his body. Even without an autopsy, it was clear to doctors and investigators that heart failure was not the cause of Saito's death. In efforts to keep himself out of the blame for the incident, it was even highly suggested to Saito's family by his stable master, Yamamoto, that Saito's body should be cremated.

It took a lawyer, who represents Japanese athletes, fighting for the rights that Saito deserved to get the police's attention to actually examine Saito's body in the first place. It had appeared at that time that the police would do anything to protect the reputation of sumo wrestling. When Saito's father saw the wounds on his son, he knew that there was something seriously wrong with his son. Thanks to pressure from the media and Saito's family, the police opened the investigation.

The Charges

In the investigation, it was found that shock from a beating had caused Saito's heart to stop. The investigation found that Yamamoto had hit Saito ten times with a beer bottle following a dinner on June 25, 2007, and then ordered three of his fellow wrestlers to beat him with a wooden stick. Yamamoto admitted to hitting Saito on the head with a beer bottle after he attempted to run away from the stable. The investigations findings further showed that Saito's body had also showed signs of being hit with a metal baseball bat. Saito also had many scars from being pricked with the burning ends of cigarettes.

Yamamoto's defense tried to say that the boys were not told to attack Saito, and that they had done that on their own initiative based on customs and trends and regular practice in the sport.

The court accepted what the prosecutors' found and stated that Yamamoto had ordered the attack on Saito and that a sparring had taken place on the second day of Saito's abuse. That second day of abuse, the court deemed, deviated far from the realm of normal stable practice and disciplines. The judge said that it was indeed the two days of physical abuse to Saito that lead to his unfortunate death.

On October 5, the Japan Sumo Association, for reasons they claimed as "severely damaging public trust", suspended Yamamoto. Yamamoto was the second stable master that had ended up banned from the sport since the Japan Sumo Association was formed in 1920s.

The Nagoya District Court sentenced Junichi Yamamoto to six years in prison for his role in the death of Takashi Saito. Three wrestlers from the stable were arrested in connection to the beating of Saito. The three wrestlers were charged with manslaughter. In the instance of the case of Saito's death, the Japan Sumo Association also punished themselves by cutting their own salaries for a few months.

So What Is Next?

Even more questions were raised after the incident on the culture of the sport of wrestling in Japan. For more than 2,000 years, sumo wrestling has been an extremely profitable profession for Japan. The bullying and hazing that is seen in the sport, beyond the death of Saito are not unique to the sport or the stables where the wrestlers live and train. In sumo, bullying is called "kiai-ire" or instilling spirit and the wrestlers refer to it as "petting".

The case put the way that new wrestlers are trained on blast in the media and in public opinion, which in turn raised many questions about customs and traditions of the sport. The Japan Sumo Association approved 87 new trainees in 2006, which is a severe drop in comparison to its peak of 223 in 1992. Wrestlers began to not show up to their traditional induction exams more often than not, and that in turn forced the Japan Sumo Association to cancel the testing of recruits.

There had been other scandals associated with the sport during that time period which included bout-fixing and marijuana use, along with many other illegal activities. The scandals continuously keep the sport in the public perception as a troubled sport with violence that actually has nothing to do with the violence that goes on in the training and matches.

The abuse and beatings that are seen in the sport of wrestling are consistent with those that were seen in the Japanese military before World War II. Following the death of Saito, many Japanese parents withdrew their kids from the Japanese wrestling schools. However, that did not actually hurt the sports participation levels as it made room for international students to come to the Japanese schools.

The increase of international students participating in the schools ended up hurting the sport's popularity within Japan, the sport's home country. Young Japanese men, who grow up intertwined in the culture of sumo wrestling have begun to reject the sport because of the brutal training and living lifestyles in the stables that are a part of sport. Many wrestlers who intended to train for sumo ended up pulling out of those intentions after Tokitaizan's death.

Those trends in the sport, the poor perception from the public and more lead to many changes in the legislation and rules of the organization.

Tokitsuumi, a Makuuchi division wrestler, took over the Tokitsukaze stable following the dismissal of Yamamoto. The Japan Sumo Association granted Tokitsuumi the change in the leadership of the stable. Tokitsuumi had to end his wrestling career early in order to take over coaching the stable, but vowed to ensure that nothing like the unfortunate incident that happened with Saito would ever happen again.

Gambling on Baseball

The Hit King. Charlie Hustle. Pete Rose.
Whatever nickname he may have had, Pete Rose
was one of the best in his profession as a major
league baseball player. His baseball career has
the statistics and records to back up that he was
one of the best. Multiple personal record
achievements in his career keeps his name
freckled throughout the history books. Pete Rose
was born in Cincinnati, Ohio in 1941. He
graduated from Western Hills High School, and
shortly after signed with the Cincinnati Reds.
His career was one to remember, but it was the
end of his career and after that people remember
most when he was banned from baseball for life.
But how did one of baseball's greats get banned
for life?

Baseball Career

In 1963, Pete Rose made his major league baseball debut as a player on the Cincinnati Reds. That season, he went on to be named Rookie of the Year. Rose surpassed 200 hits a total of ten times. He also won batting titles in 1968 and 1969 and two Golden Gloves in 1969 and 1970 for his outstanding defense. In 1973, Rose was named the NL Most Valuable Player.

Rose was a member of the Reds when they won back-to-back World Series Championships in 1975 and 1976 while also setting a National League 44-game hit streak in 1978. He was then traded to the Philadelphia Phillies and led them to their first World Series Championship in 1980. In 1984, Rose went to the Montreal Expos for half a season before going back to Cincinnati Reds as a player-manager. Rose was welcomed in Cincinnati with open arms, the town excited to have his talent back in their stadium. In 1985, Rose broke Ty Cobb's 57-year record number of hits - 4,912 and he went on to be named ABC Wide World of Sports Athlete of the Year. Rose's last season as a player was in 1986, ending his career with 4,256 total hits, 902 doubles, and also held the all-time records playing in 3,562 games and 14,053 at-bats.

Rose ended his career with 19 records, going on to be a manager for the Reds full-time. As a manager, he was equally successful with a 426-388 record. During that time, the Reds were in second place in the National League West division four times, from 1985-1988. His 426 total wins as a manager have him ranked fifth for the Reds history among managers.

In 1988, Rose's well-known fiery playing style got the best of him when he decided to argue with an umpire over a call. Rose made physical contact with umpire, Dave Pallone, resulting in a 30-day suspension handed down from National League President, Bart Giamatti. This was the most severe punishment given out to date for an on-field incident. The entire incident also got extremely out of hand when the fans began throwing objects onto the field at the umpires. However, on August 24, 1989, Rose's baseball life changed forever and it was in an even bigger way than he imagined.

Then Came the Scandal

It was during his time as a manager for the Cincinnati Reds that suspicions arose about Rose's gambling habits. He had a tendency to bet on horses, and was frequently seen at the racetracks. Lots of eyes turned away from a problem that was clearly evident. However, in 1989, the suspicions came out about Rose actually may have gambled on baseball. Not just betting on baseball, but at times, betting on his own team and against his own team.

Amid the suspicions, an investigation was launched by John Dowd, former Justice Department prosecutor. It was in his report, the Dowd Report, that enough evidence was found to bring down Pete Rose and his career. In Dowd's Report, there was a lot of evidence which proved that Rose gambled but Dowd was unsuccessful in proving that Rose betted on his own team. Dowd reported that there wasn't enough time to process the little bit of evidence that he found prior to releasing the report, and that more time may have proven Rose's part in betting against his team.

The evidence found against Rose was substantial. Betting slips, phone calls to bookies, every day and on nearly every single baseball team. Evidence says that nearly $20,000 a day was being waged by Rose in bets.

On August 24, 1989, Pete Rose was the 15th person to be banned for life from baseball. Giamatti held a press conference announcing the banishment and was convinced that Rose had bet on the game despite the evidence Dowd found not clearly stating otherwise. The Reds also held a press conference announcing that since Rose was banned, he could no longer be the manager. The city of Cincinnati mourned the news and let down from one of their own greats.

Black, White or Gray?

Throughout the sport of baseball, both on the field and by the fans, Rose was beloved and hated. His fiery attitude sometimes rubbed others the wrong way. He was seen as having a gambling addiction that he couldn't control, and no one close to him did anything to help him out. Addiction with gambling is held in someone's mind just as addiction with any other substance - it is hard for that person to grasp the control that is necessary for them overcome that addiction.

Others believe that he didn't have a problem, and that he was completely in control, faulting his choices and turning away from the evidence of a real problem. The entire controversy around Rose and what he did and when he did it was black and white, in some cases with plenty of gray in between.

There were those who looked up to him and defended him - his records, his fierce loyalty to his teammates and his friends, the ones who saw him as a hero on the baseball field and knew that the gambling addiction was something that he couldn't control and he needed help.

Even more controversy surrounded Rose's future in the Hall of Fame. There is no doubt that he has the records to fit the criteria, but breaking the rules of baseball eliminated the good he had contributed to the sport. Induction into the Hall of Fame has some of the highest standards for admittance, an in-depth process with a lot of discussions to decide who is in and who is out.

There was also a lot of gray area around the major league baseball commission. Since it was evident to those surrounding Rose that there was a gambling problem, many people have wondered when Commissioner Bart Giamatti knew about Rose's issue and why it was only brought to light for investigation not long after he had retired as a player.

Many baseball experts wonder if this was a way for the MLB to flex their muscles and make clear the blurred lines between the player and administration in the league - a line that during that time period, was very much scrutinized. Giamatti's lack of participation in the trial due to how poorly he performed under questioning also raised a lot of suspicion around Rose and the Scandal. Even more so, discussions and arguments were made because of how many members of the Hall of Fame at that time were gamblers, addicts and steroid-users.

The Issue Remains

Then in 2004, many years after the scandal had been put to rest Rose publicly confessed to betting on baseball. He authored an autobiography, My Prison Without Bars, which goes in depth to his personal life, finally admitting the errors that he had done throughout his life. He confronts the issues that he has had with gambling, giving the reader insight into what it was like for him to struggle through his demons.

The questions still remain to this day, the biggest one being - does someone who breaks the rules of the league still deserve a spot in the Hall of Fame that the record books say he earned? Is a personal problem off the field enough to erase someone's achievements on the field? How does the governing body know when to interfere when a personal problem has the possibility to interfere with the integrity of the sport? How much time is enough for someone to serve their sentence of banishment to be let back in the league? Or, is it truly a forever conversation? Who is right in saying that some offenses are lesser than others when rules are clearly broken?

There is no denying that Rose was a fantastic baseball player - one of the greats. Some say that he would be comparable to Jeter and Ichiro if he was playing in present day. As experts, players and the media struggle to answer those questions with baseball scandals today, Pete Rose sits back and waits for his spot in the Hall of Fame that he believes he deserves. Until then, he signs autographs on memorabilia for those who still believe in him.

2002 Winter Olympic Bid Scandal

Hosting an Olympic games in your own country and city is one of the biggest honors for all of sporting events and competition. As the host city, you have the opportunity to educate the world about your country and its culture, and the chance to support your own athletes in their own backyard. The eyes of the world are on that host city for several weeks, even months; the media is scrutinizing the city's every move and everyone around the world is counting on the ability to cheer on their own athletes as they compete. To earn the honor of hosting the Olympics, there is a competitive bid process that any interested country must endure. The 2002 Winter Olympics bid was an eye opener into that process, but not for the right reasons.

The Bidding Process

The Olympic Games, along with the honor of hosting them, is an extremely complex production – thousands of athletes, coaches, spectators, media and more are all in one location, and the logistics from space to have the competitions to where people can stay takes many years of planning, construction and logistical preparation. There are many different organizations, authorities and stakeholders involved that must all be working together in order for the games to run smoothly. For a city to earn the honor of hosting the Olympic Games over all of the others who choose to enter, there are several criteria and steps involved in the bidding process to properly vet a location.

Overall, the entire bidding process is about two years long. The International Olympic Committee (IOC) is made up of key Olympic stakeholders and manages the selection for the host city for the Olympic Games. Seven years before those games are going to take place, the host city is announced but that is after they go through a two year bidding process. In the first phase of the two year bidding process, a potential host city goes through an applicant phase. The second phase is called the candidature phase. In the applicant phase, potential host cities must submit an application file to the International Olympic Committee for further consideration. From that point, there are only a few cities that move on from the candidate phase to the candidature phase. In the candidature phase, cities under consideration must submit even more detailed information and plans, strengths and weaknesses, for them to be considered the host city.

The IOC Evaluation Commission will visit each city and produce important risk assessments, along with the strengths and weaknesses of all cities under consideration. Following many presentations and in-depth explanation of the host cities reasoning for being chosen, the IOC members will vote on the host city that will host the Olympic Games and then sign a contract with the IOC.

Extremely thorough and very long, the Olympic Games hosting process takes a lot of time, energy and planning to have the honor of welcoming athletes from all over the world into your home. To think that there would be people who would take advantage of that honor on behalf of a great payout is hard to believe, but unfortunately, it has happened all too many times.

Corruption Strikes

In December 1998, corruption, confusion and many questions were raised when a senior International Olympic Committee official said that bribes from cities looking to host the 2002 games were up to nearly one million dollars between four people that were promising votes for payments. The group of four involved in bidding for votes received amounts between $500,000 and one million, and that the winning city would have to pay between three million to five million dollars. That same senior International Olympic Committee official also let it be known that there was also bribing and voting that went on for the 1996 games for Atlanta, Sydney for the 2000 Olympic Games and Salt Lake City for the 2002 Winter Olympic Games. In all, nearly 30 of the International Olympic Committee's 114 delegates of that time period have had some sort of hand in bidding and conspiracy with the cities trying to host the Olympic Games.

When allegations came to light that the selection for the Salt Lake City 2002 Winter Olympics did not follow the honorable process that cities before them had followed, the International Olympic Committee quickly launched an investigation of their own into the allegations.

Specifically with the Salt Lake City 2002 Winter Olympics, two chief organizers were indicted by a federal grand jury under the suspicion and charges that there was conspiracy and bribery involved in the bidding process for the games.

What Went Down

Many people were involved in bringing and conspiracy to conceal the host for the 2002 Winter Olympic Games. Allegedly, Thomas Welch, the former president of the Salt Lake City bid committee, and vice president, David Johnson, had paid more than one million dollars to influence votes in their favor. Through their bribery of $1 million, they aimed to sway more than a dozen members of the International Olympic Committee.

To conceal how they were operating in bribing members of the International Olympic Committee, Thomas Welch and David Johnson secretly paid a member of the United States Olympic Committee to assist them in winning the bid for the 2002 Winter Olympic Games. From false contracts, to bookkeeping records and other important documents used in the bidding process, it was concealed almost perfectly that money was being exchanged for votes to select the host site of Salt Lake City as the most qualified city to have the games in that location.

Investigation Findings & Results

Due to how early host sites are selected for the Olympics because of the length of the entire bidding process, the scandal truly came to light in 1998 and 1999, damaging the honorable and prestigious process that a city must go through in order to have the honor of hosting either the Winter or Summer Olympic Games. Especially damaging was the reputation of the committee that is responsible for selecting the host site for the Olympic Games. Four separate investigations were launched into the bribery allegations that were brought to light by Marc Holder. Internal investigations also took place with the Salt Lake Olympic Committee, the US Olympic Committee and the IOC to see who on the inside was aware of any wrongdoings.

Within the investigations and the findings that came about, Welch and Johnson are most tightly tied to being the ones who planned to win votes with money and payouts to the International Olympic Committee. In all, a total of ten members of the International Olympic Committee resigned or were forced to resign due to the information that came to light in the scandal.

The final findings from the ethics panel responsible for investigation the scandal concluded that more than $1.2 million in cash, scholarships, jobs, medical treatment, shopping and travel expenses went to members of the International Olympic Committee and even extended to their families. Some findings revealed that one of the Salt Lake City Olympic Committee members contributed to a campaign for one of the IOC members who was running for mayor in Santiago, Chile. Other findings revealed that they provided college tuition for the children of members from Ecuador and Libya. Cash contributions also went out to many of the other members in the IOC.

When it comes to countries that consistently have a lower chance of winning an Olympic host city bid, they are easy targets for having their votes bought by more powerful cities and countries.

During the trials, both Welch and Johnson continuously denied that they were guilty of any of the allegations. When they were finally charged, they received one count of conspiracy, five counts of mail fraud, five counts of wire fraud, four counts of interstate travel in racketeering and one count of using money for personal purposes. Those charges each resulted in a five-year maximum sentence in prison and a fine of $250,000.

Surprising? Only For Some

Although to the general public it may have come as a massive shock that there was bribery and conspiracy involved in selecting a host city, it wasn't as much of a shock for others. The corporate involvement in this Olympic scandal was a trend that has been on the rise with Olympic bidding since the end of World War II. Especially considering the international tension that remained following the conclusion of World War II, the American efforts to win a bid dishonorably did not help.

To ensure that they fight the possibility of corruption tainting the selection of the host for the Olympic Games again, the International Olympic Committee set in place several new policies and procedures. One of those policies, the prohibition of how much members of the International Olympic Committee could accept from bid cities, limits to the terms and ages of the committee members and stricter guidance around what actions are acceptable around people looking to win a host city bid. The changes in place strive to ensure that scandal to this scale doesn't leave another scar on the Olympics.

Made in the USA
Monee, IL
21 December 2021